CONTENTS

The Day After Tomorrow   9

The Girl with the Banana   14

The Bean Thieves   21

The New Nose   25

The Rough Diamond   30

The House by the Sea   35

Dancing in the Dark   40

The Big Black Box   46

The Big Idea   51

The Newspaper Seller   56

The Harvest Envelope   61

ALL GOD'S CHILDREN

Jesus said to them,
'let the children come to me;
do not try to stop them;
for the Kingdom of Heaven
belongs to such as these.'

Matthew 19:14

Pauline M. Webb

MARSHALL, MORGAN & SCOTT

LAKELAND
Marshall, Morgan & Scott
a member of the Pentos group
1 Bath Street, London EC1V 9LB

© Marshall, Morgan & Scott, 1964 and 1978
First Published 1964
This abridged edition 1978

ISBN 0 551 00779 6

Printed in Great Britain by
J. W. Arrowsmith Ltd, Bristol
8710L01

Hello boys and girls,

My favourite stories are always true stories about real people. So this is a book of stories about children I or some of my friends have actually met, in many different parts of the world. One of the exciting things about travelling abroad is that wherever you go you can meet friendly people, and I find that the most friendly of all are boys and girls. They seem to know a secret which many grown-ups need to learn. They know that it makes no difference what country we come from, what language we speak or what colour we are. We can make friends with people from every country, we can smile at each other in any language, we can join hands with children of all races. We all really belong to one family, because we are all God's children. So I hope you will enjoy reading these stories about your brothers and sisters in other places, and that you will learn to make friends with many more boys and girls who have come to live in our country from other lands, so that you can show grown-ups too what it means to live in peace and love one another.

God bless you all,

PAULINE M. WEBB

The Day After Tomorrow

No-one knew why Otunla was called 'The Day After Tomorrow', but that was really what his name meant. In the place where he lived in Nigeria, children were usually called after the day of the week on which they were born, so one boy's name would mean 'Monday' and another's 'Tuesday' and so on. But for some reason Otunla had been called 'The Day After Tomorrow', and as he grew up, everyone said the name exactly suited him. 'Come on, Otunla', his mother would call in the morning. 'It's time to get up. It's no use thinking you can stay there sleeping until the day after tomorrow!' By the time he had at last got up from his sleeping mat and put on his shorts and combed his hair, she would be calling again. 'Come on, Otunla, hurry up – I want you to come down to the well with me to help me carry the water home. The day after tomorrow won't do, you know!' Then, when they had fetched the water, she would want him to go with her to the market. It was a long, long way to walk, and Otunla would dawdle behind till his mother called 'Get a move on, Otunla. At your rate, we shan't be there until the day after tomorrow!' Sometimes, he would have to help to chop up firewood for his mother's cooking fire, and he would

be so slow about it that his mother would call, 'Do you
want your dinner today or the day after tomorrow?
That's when it will be if you don't work more quickly
than this.'

Otunla never did hurry over anything, because he
was always dreaming about what he would do on the
day after tomorrow, when he was grown up and could
do just what he liked. Sometimes he thought he would
be a farmer like his father, but more often he wished
that he could go right away from the village altogether
and go to live in a big city, like the one he had heard
about called Lagos. One of the boys who had gone
there from the village had come back and told Otunla
that Lagos was a wonderful place. People didn't have
to go to the well there, because there were houses in
Lagos where the water came out of taps. There was no
need to chop firewood, because some people had electric
stoves to cook on. You didn't even have to walk very
far, because there were fast cars and big roads to race
along and splendid shops.

Otunla used to sit and dream about the big city and
wonder how he would ever get there. His friend told
him that he could get him a job there. Many of the
people living in Lagos had servants working in their
houses, and he promised Otunla that he could fix him up
as a cook-boy in a rich man's house, and then later on he
could find another job and make a lot of money and be
a rich man himself.

So Otunla started trying to persuade his father to
give him the fare and let him go to Lagos to seek his
fortune. His mother and father didn't want him to go

away from home at all, but Otunla argued so much that in the end, his father agreed, and Otunla set out, full of hope and excitement to go off to the big city and the bright lights and the splendid shops.

It was not a very comfortable journey at first bumping along the rough road from Otunla's village in the rickety old lorry. But that was the only bus there was and it had a good motto printed on the front, 'Tomorrow never comes'. When they reached the main road the lorry sped along so fast that Otunla was really rather frightened and was relieved when at last they arrived safely in Lagos.

He was glad that his friend was there to meet him, because Lagos itself was even more frightening. The shops were so very big and the traffic so fast that Otunla hardly dared cross the road. At last they got to a quieter part of the town where there were some very big houses and where his friend introduced him to a family who were wanting a cook-boy, and they agreed to take him on.

He wasn't a very good cook-boy. He was so dreamy that he often let things burn in the shining bright oven, and then his mistress would be cross and scold him far more angrily than his mother ever did. He wasn't used to turning taps off either, so often the water flooded all over the kitchen and he would be in trouble again. He even got muddled up in the cooking, and put sugar instead of salt into the stew and custard powder instead of cornflour into the sauce, until his master was so angry that he lost his job. Then he was very sad in the great city, because he had no job, no money and no-one to care about him. He dared not go back home because he was sure his father and mother would be angry with him.

Then, as he wandered along one of the main streets of the city he heard the sound of people singing. They sounded so happy, and so Otunla stopped to listen. The music was coming from a great stone building on the other side of the road. The doors were wide open, because it was so hot that the people wanted to keep as cool as they could. So it was easy to hear what was happening inside the building, which was a big church. Otunla darted across between the traffic and crept up to the doorway. Just as he got there, the singing ended and the people sat down. Then an African minister began reading a story in Otunla's own language. It was all about a boy who had left home to go to a far country, and who had lost all his money and wanted to go back home again. He had been almost afraid to go, but as he got near to his home, his father was so glad to see him back that he came running to meet him and made a great feast for him.

Otunla felt a great lump come into his throat when he heard that story. He knew just how that boy felt, because he was so homesick too. He stopped to listen while the minister preached to the people and said that the love of God was like the love of that father. Otunla couldn't understand that, because he had never heard anything about the love of God before, but he did know he wanted more than anything else in the world to go home where he had a mother and father who loved him.

After the service, the minister came to talk to Otunla and asked him what he was doing there. When he heard the story, he said, 'Otunla, I'm going to take you back home again.'

So Otunla went back to his own village, leaving behind him all the bright lights and the big streets and the fast cars, and travelling with the minister in his car back along the bumpy road to his old village.

Somehow, the lamp burning in his own home looked brighter than all the lights of the city, and the ground-nut stew his mother cooked for him was the best food he had tasted for weeks. The minister stayed to talk with his parents and told them how sad Otunla had been in the city and how glad he was to come home again. He said that he hoped he would be able to come and visit Otunla's village often and teach all the people there much more about the love of God. Then, before he left Otunla, he gave him just this one word of advice about his adventure. 'Remember Otunla, that instead of dreaming all the time about the day after tomorrow it is better to enjoy all the good things God has given you today.'

The Girl with the Banana

Packiam was so hungry that when the doctor gave her a banana to eat, she couldn't wait even to take the peel off, but tried straight away to gobble it all up. You might think that she must have been a very greedy girl, but then you have probably never been so hungry as she was.

You see, Packiam was born in a village in India at a time when there had been no rain for six whole years. That meant that there was nothing at all growing in the fields. The ground was caked dry and as hard as a rock. The wells were dried up. All the people were hungry. The little children cried for food all day long, but they thought they were fortunate if their mothers could find enough food to give them a meal three times a week. So Packiam, whose name means 'Happiness', was never really happy at all because she was always hungry.

When she was still a very small child, her mother and father left the famine village to try to find food somewhere else. They thought there might be some place where rain had fallen and where people had good stocks of grain and where there was work so that they could earn money to buy food. They had taken Packiam with them and everywhere they went, they begged people to give them something to eat. As soon as Packiam could toddle, they had taught her to beg too. Then, they thought people would take more pity on a little girl alone. So they left her, while they went off further in search of food, hoping to come back and find her one day. She had an old, empty coconut shell for a begging bowl and she would hold it out in front of her, lisping the one word, 'Passi, passi,' which means 'I'm hungry, I'm hungry.'

Being only a small girl of four years old she didn't look after herself very well. She soon became dirty and bedraggled, and her dress was badly torn. Her hair was knotted and straggly and she always looked so unhappy that people thought she was an ugly little urchin and no-one took much notice of her as she wandered from place to place begging everywhere. She would wait near the shrine at the entrance to a village, where people came to bring their offerings. Then they would toss a handful of rice or even sometimes some sweetmeats into her bowl, and they would be rewarded with a flash of a bright smile as she grabbed hold of the food quickly and crammed it into her mouth before any crumbs could fall.

One day she reached a village she had never been in before. She went to look for the shrine, but to her surprise she found that it was quite empty. So she decided to go further into the village and see whether she could find anyone to give her food. There were not many people about. The grown-ups all seemed to be out in the fields working, and the children were nowhere to be seen. Only big dogs prowled about, and they, like Packiam, were looking for something to eat. There was one house that was a bit bigger than the others, and as Packiam went towards it she could hear such a noise that she guessed that this was where all the village children must be. Sure enough, there they were, sitting on the floor on the verandah of this large house, learning lessons from a blackboard. It was a Christian school.

Packiam was just going up closer to them, when she saw nearby a little heap of big banana leaves, and on top was one which still had some scraps of rice on it. These must have been the leaf-plates from which the children had just had their meal. Quickly, before any-one could see her, she darted forward to seize hold of the rice. But something else moved even more quickly than she did! One of the big dogs dashed out and bit into her arm so hard that she had to let go of the rice, and fell back in the dust, trying not to cry out from the pain.

The children had all heard the scuffle and stopped their work to come and see what had happened. Packiam tried to scramble to her feet and scurry away quickly but before she had time to pick herself up the teacher came over to her and lifted her up in his strong arms and carried her into the shade of the verandah. There was something very comforting about those arms and as Packiam looked up through her tears she saw kind eyes smiling down at her and felt his hands smoothing her hair, as he comforted her in a soft, quiet voice. Then he spoke to the children for a few minutes, giving them work to do, while he took Packiam along to a building in the village which looked to her like a big hall. Many people were waiting there. He told her it was really their church, but today it was being used as a clinic.

He carried Packiam up to the front of the church to a place where a lady in a white sari was sitting at a table. 'Please could you take this little girl to the hospital?' he said. 'She has been badly bitten by a dog, but she also seems very weak and hungry and there doesn't seem to be anyone to take care of her.'

The lady in the white sari stretched out her arms to take Packiam on to her knee, but she clung shyly to her new friend and refused to be parted from him. Then the lady picked out a banana from a bag on the table and tried to coax Packiam with that. At the sight of food, Packiam immediately grabbed out and tried to cram the banana straight into her mouth. The lady laughed, and peeled it for her and then asked her what her name was.

Packiam's mouth was so full of banana that she could hardly speak, but she managed to say 'Packiam' and, as she always did, she went on to say, 'Passi, I'm hungry.' 'Well, Packiam', said the lady, 'we must see if we can make you look as happy as your name.'

Then she examined Packiam's arm carefully and called a nurse over to her to take Packiam and wash her arm with cool lotion and bandage it so that it would feel clean and comfortable. 'And while I'm seeing the rest of the patients,' said the doctor, 'you can give her something to eat and drink.'

So Packiam had her first really good meal. Then, when the doctor was ready, for the first time in her life she had a ride in a big van, going back to the hospital with the doctor and the nurses and all the medicines. It was a long journey from the village, and by the time they had jolted over the rough lanes, Packiam was fast asleep. When she woke up again, she was lying in bed, with a clean white sheet over her. Someone raised her head and sweet, warm milk began to trickle down her throat.

That was good, but soon other strange things began to happen. She stayed in the hospital for many weeks. She was washed and scrubbed until her face glowed and her skin tingled. Her hair was brushed and combed until it was sleek and smooth. They gave her good food until her limbs began to fill out and grow strong. Every day a teacher came to tell the children a special story about Jesus and how He had cared for people. Packiam liked best the one about the way in which He had fed the hungry people with loaves and fishes. She learned to sing songs too, and sometimes she would begin to play with some of the other children in the ward. But she was never really happy. She was always afraid that one day she would be sent away and one day she would be hungry again.

No-one did send her away again. Instead, when she was quite well and her wounds had healed, the van took Packiam from the hospital into the hills where there was a beautiful house. There were many other children there who had once been lost as she was, but who were now being loved by Christian people who cared for them in

a Children's Home. So Packiam has joined their family
and now she really has found happiness. She is not
afraid any more because now she has found love.

The Bean Thieves

It was early morning, and in one of the small harbours on the island of Haiti in the West Indies people had not yet woken up to begin the day's work. A few small boats were tied up by the wharf, and along the landing-stage stood the bulging great sacks which had been unloaded the day before and were to be carted off to other parts of the island later on that day. A solitary policeman tramped up and down along the quay-side, keeping a watchful eye on things. There was no-one else in sight except for a small car parked up by the side of the wharf, where the local minister was waiting to meet a motor-boat due to bring in some supplies for his church that morning.

The minister looked around him lazily, thinking how calm and quiet everything looked. The sea lay peaceful, the trees rustled so lightly that there could hardly be any breeze at all. It seemed impossible to realise that only a few weeks ago in this very same place the wind had come howling in with such tremendous force that tidal waves had flooded over the island, sweeping away houses and trees, destroying crops and cattle, and even killing many thousands of people in one of the worst hurricanes in living memory. Then, as suddenly as it had come, Hurricane 'Hazel' had gone away again, leaving behind such havoc that it would be a long time before all the people had homes to live in again and enough food to eat. But the minister hoped that the supplies he was waiting for that very morning would go some way towards helping them. Every day, almost, special relief supplies of food were arriving from America, sent by Church World Service, to be given to some of the very many children who would otherwise have died of starvation. Some of these supplies would go to a little home which one of the church members had opened for sick mothers and children. Some would go to the small hospital. Some would go to families which the minister knew himself, where they were finding it very hard to buy food.

He was just planning out how he would give it all away, when suddenly he saw someone moving in the shadows along the wharf. Very quietly and quickly, a little figure was darting in and out between the big wooden bollards there, making his way towards the place where the great sacks were standing on the quay-side. Suddenly the policeman turned round and started moving towards the sacks, and immediately the little figure disappeared from sight. He must have crouched down so low that he was hiding right behind the sack. As soon as the policeman turned his back again, the minister saw a little head appear above the sack and a small hand beckoned eagerly to others to come and join him. Then, as if by magic, from all sides small boys began to appear and creep up to the sacks.

The minister watched carefully to see what they would

do. The first boy looked around him very carefully, and then, thinking that no-one was watching him, he poked his finger hard into the biggest sack and wiggled it about until he had made quite a large hole. Then, one after the other the boys came with small tin cans which they held under the hole while the leader poked the sack to make the beans come trickling out.

Then, suddenly, while they were intent on what they were doing, the policeman turned round and saw them. 'Stop thief' he shouted and blew hard on his whistle as he started chasing after them. But the boys were quicker on their feet than he was and in no time they had given him the slip and disappeared from sight. 'The wicked little thieves!' muttered the policeman, as he wiped his brow. 'They're at it again. Every morning it's the same. As soon as my back is turned, down they come, stealing whatever they can find on the wharf. One of these days when I catch them, I'll give them such a thrashing that they'll never try to steal again as long as they live.'

'Where do they come from?' asked the minister.

'Most of them don't come from anywhere in particular', said the policeman. 'Most of them lost their homes and their parents in the hurricane and now they haven't anywhere to live or anyone to look after them. Some of them live with aunts or uncles in shacks in the town; some just sleep in the canoes on the beach. But wherever they live they get their food by stealing and that is quite wrong and I've got to stop it.'

The minister agreed, of course, that it was wrong for the boys to steal, but he longed to be able to do something to help them. So each morning he went down to the wharf, hoping that somehow or other he would be able to get to know the boys and find out what he could do for them.

At first, he couldn't get near them at all. Every time they saw him coming and he went towards them, they scurried away, thinking he was another policeman. So instead, he just waited by the wharf where they could see him and where they would know that he could see them. Every day he saw them doing the same thing, creeping down to the wharf, and helping themselves to any kind of food that was standing about there. Though he was very sad that they had to steal like that, he waited for a few days before he said anything to them. Gradually, they got used to the idea that he wasn't going to chase them or punish them and at last they let him talk to them and become their friend.

Then he told them that if they came up to his church every day, he would try to have a meal ready for them so that they need not steal. The Sunday School teachers and the women in the church had all promised that they would help to run a small canteen, and the Church World Service and the government had said they would provide the food. So every day, fifteen little boys who used to be harbour thieves began going to church.

At first, they went there only because there was food for them to eat. Soon they found that there were people at the church who cared about them too and wanted them to grow up as good and honest boys. Then they began to tell other boys too about this wonderful place where people cared about the hungry children. So more and more of them started coming to church to have one good meal every day. The people have built a new little hall especially for them, and the children enjoy meeting in their brightly-coloured, gaily painted dining room. Because the room is so fresh and clean, they are trying to keep themselves clean and tidy too.

When they first started coming to the canteen, the children were very rough and sometimes even greedy. There were so afraid of being hungry again that they would snatch all the food they could, and even try to carry some away with them. But now they are learning how to serve each other at table, and how to wait at the beginning of their meal while they sing their 'thank-you' grace and then start their meal together. The people who prepare the meal make sure that it is good and nourishing food, so that the boys are becoming much stronger and healthier than they were when the minister first met them.

The biggest change of all is that they are learning that there are people in the world whom they can trust and who trust them. So they do not try to steal any more. Some of them have begun coming to church not only for their meal, but also for Sunday School as well. There they are learning to love Jesus because other people have loved them.

The New Nose

John could tell from the way that other children looked at him that there must be something wrong with his face. Whenever they got very near to him they would look hard, and then hurry away without even speaking to him. It was difficult to understand at first, because there had been a time when everyone seemed to like him and want to play with him. But now all his old friends avoided him and sometimes he was sure he could hear them whispering behind his back and pointing at him from a long way off.

He was almost afraid to ask anyone what was the matter, because he could nearly guess. In India, where he lived, he knew that some people were always avoided because they showed signs of having a disease which is dreaded almost more than any other disease there is, the disease of leprosy. Yet John did not really feel ill. It was only his face that showed any mark, and he could not see that himself because in the house where he lived there wasn't any mirror. He couldn't even feel anything either, except that sometimes when he put his hand up to his face, it felt as though his nose was getting flatter against his face, without a proper bridge to it. But he couldn't feel any pain, and he hadn't had any accident, so perhaps it was only his imagination. He just hoped there was nothing seriously wrong.

One day, however, he thought he ought to make sure. He knew that usually one day a week a doctor came to their village, so he thought he would go and see what he advised. As soon as the doctor saw him, John could tell that he thought there really was something very seriously wrong. He made some tests and then said he wanted John to go to the special hospital at Dichpalli where they would be able to tell definitely whether he had leprosy or not.

So John and his mother went together on a long train journey to Dichpalli. He was very nervous indeed, especially when he arrived there and saw what a big place it was. There seemed to be hundreds of people about and all of them were busy. Some were working in the fields, some were preparing food, some were chopping wood, some were making baskets, and some were waiting in a long, long queue outside the doctor's room. That was the queue which John and his mother had to join and while they were waiting he looked around him a bit. It didn't look at all like he had imagined a hospital to be. There seemed to be rows and rows of small houses, as well as a large hall, where he could see some boys about his own age doing exercises. Then there was a building that looked like a chapel, and nearby a large block with offices and rooms like the one where he would see the doctor. The only place that looked at all like a hospital was a building where he could see a man being wheeled along a corridor on a stretcher, as though he had just come back from an operation.

By the time it came to John's turn to be examined, he had become quite interested in all the things going on around him. He was especially interested in the tests the doctor made on his own skin. First he told John to close his eyes while he touched different parts of John's skin with a piece of cotton wool, and John had to tell him where he felt the touch. In some places it was easy, but there were some times when he felt nothing at all. Then the doctor took scrapings from John's skin and looked at them through a microscope. After a little while he said, 'Yes, you quite clearly have caught leprosy, but there's nothing to be afraid of. If you can come here and stay we will do all we can to treat you and make you better.' 'How long must I stay here?' asked John. 'That we can't say' said the doctor. 'It may be a very long time, but we will try and make life here as happy as it can be.'

He asked John for his name and the village he came from. When he heard the name 'John', he said 'So you are a Christian then. You will be very happy here, for this is a Christian hospital and you will be able to share in all the Christian service here.'

John's mother was sad to have to leave him for such a long time, but she could see that he would be well looked after, and they told her she could come and visit him often, so she went away happily.

John soon settled down very well at Dichpalli. There were so many things to do there. He was able to go to school. He belonged to the football team. He joined the Boys' Brigade. He helped on the farm. Every day he went for his treatment, which meant having tablets

and then going to do special exercises to keep his fingers
and feet active and strong. Yet for a long, long time,
over four years, he didn't seem to get any better. What
worried him most was that sometimes when he was in
the clinic watching patients, whose hands were crippled,
having their hands put into the wax bath which helped
them to do their exercises, he would catch a sight of his
own face in the gleaming instruments in front of him,
and he could see that his nose had indeed fallen quite
flat, as the bridge bone had gradually collapsed. He
shuddered to see how ugly he had become.

Yet at the hospital no-one else seemed to worry about
his appearance. John was a very popular boy indeed
and everyone was glad when the tests began to show
that at last he was getting better. In fact, one day when
he went to have a check-up, the doctor said to him,
'Well, John, I think we shall soon be able to send you
home again. You haven't got leprosy any longer!'

The doctor expected John to be delighted, but to his
surprise John looked dismayed. 'What is worrying you?'
asked the doctor. 'Don't you want to go home?'

Then John stammered out an explanation. 'I – I am
afraid to go back, sir. The other boys will think that I
am ugly and will laugh at my face because it has
become so damaged by leprosy.'

'I understand,' said the doctor, 'and I will see what
we can do.'

A few weeks later, John learnt that he was to be a
patient in one of the wards of the hospital. He had not
had to stay in bed at all while he had been at Dichpalli,
but now they told him he was going to have an opera-

tion and that would mean spending a few hours in the operating theatre and then a few days in bed. 'We're going to make you a new nose,' the doctor explained.

John didn't remember anything about the operation of course, because he was asleep through it all. What did surprise him, though, when he woke up was to find that his leg, as well as his face, was in bandages. The surgeon had been able to build him a new nose by taking a little bit of bone out of his leg! So, for a while he limped a bit, but by the time he had recovered from the operation, he had a brand new face and no-one could tell that there had been anything wrong.

Then came the great day when John was at last allowed to go home again. There was a very special Thanksgiving Service in the chapel, where John received from the doctor the most wonderful gift he had ever had, a piece of paper which said he was quite free from leprosy. Then the minister read the story of how Jesus had once cured ten men from leprosy, and one of them had come back to thank Him. But John felt that he would never stop being thankful to that Christian hospital and the surgeon and all the people who had cared for him, so that now he could go back to his friends and meet them face to face, without being afraid of anyone any more.

The Rough Diamond

Ratnam's name means 'Jewel', but some people might call him a rough diamond, because he looked very rough and he was always up to mischief. In the Indian village where he lived, no-one had much time to bother about keeping boys in order. Everyone had to work in the fields. Only the children were left with nothing much to do except chase one another up and down the crooked passageways between the mud thatched houses, which were huddled so closely together that it was easy to hide between them and then leap out and frighten the person who was doing the chasing.

Ratnam had his own special ways of getting into mischief. One thing he liked to do was to make the girls jump by pretending to pull a snake across their path. It wasn't really a snake, of course. It was only one he had made himself, by getting a long strip of old newspaper and folding it into a concertina shape. For a head he used a piece of twig with a length of cotton wound round it, so that when he pulled the cotton, the snake seemed to wriggle forward all on its own.

Another trick he had was with his own special bow and arrow. He made this out of a flat piece of wood with a hole bored in it. For the string of the bow he got an old piece of bicycle tube rubber, and stretched it over the ends of the wood. Then he made arrows from pieces of bamboo split at the ends, with a tailpiece of newspaper slotted into them. By fitting the arrows between the hole in the bow and the rubber, he could let them fly wherever he wanted. Sometimes, just as someone was bending over low in the rice-fields, with his back to the village, there would be a loud ping! The arrow would come flying, but before the victim could look round and see who had shot him, Ratnam was nowhere to be seen.

His best toy of all was his special whistle. He had made this out of a hollow piece of bamboo, into which he had notched holes so that he could play different notes by covering them with his fingers, just like a recorder. He used this for mischief too sometimes. Just when the men had come in from the fields and were lying down for a quiet nap in the shade of their houses, Ratnam would creep along and blow his whistle right in their ears, so that it sounded almost like a trumpet call waking them up again!

So everyone in the village was very glad when they heard that Ratnam's family were moving away to live in a town many miles away. His father had a new job in a factory and he wanted to take his wife and children with him to live in the new town. Ratnam's mother was delighted with their new little tiled house in one of the long straight rows of the factory estate. But Ratnam was not so delighted when he heard that now, instead of playing about all day, he would be able to go to school, in a small hall beside the church in the town.

From the very first day he went there, Ratnam decided that he did not like school at all. He hated having to sit in a row of other boys and do exactly what the teachers said. What he hated most was that the other boys had been at school much longer than he had, and so they had learned a lot more. They were all able to read and write and do sums, but Ratnam was quite hopeless in all his lessons. What was even worse, the others looked down on him because he came from a village. They thought he was good-for-nothing and quite useless. Ratnam became so unhappy that he decided he just would not go to school any more.

So one day, when he heard the school-bell ringing, he left home and deliberately went off in the opposite direction. He didn't really know the town very well, and it was very confusing, because all the long streets of houses looked much the same. He dared not go any-where near the factory, because he was afraid his father might see him and know he had not gone to school. He dared not go back home, because he knew his mother would be very angry. So he decided to find a place where he could wait all day and watch carefully until the children came out of school again and go home with them. There was only one place for that, he thought – he would climb up a tree.

High up among the branches, he was quite comfort-able for a time. He grew hungry, of course, but he was used to that, because back home in the village there had often been days when there had not been enough food to spare for a meal during the day. But up there in the tree, the day seemed very long indeed, so he decided to try and cheer himself up a bit. He took out his whistle and began playing a little tune. He had only picked out the first four notes when he heard someone shout 'There he is! There's Ratnam. That's his whistle.' He looked down, and there at the foot of the tree stood his teacher and a group of boys from his class. They had all come out during the break to look for him!

Sheepishly he clambered down the tree and waited for the scolding he was sure he would get.

To his surprise as they walked back to school the first thing the teacher said was, 'That's a fine whistle, Ratnam. Where did you get it from?' 'Made it myself' he muttered, looking down on the ground and kicking a stone as hard as he could. 'Do you often make things?' asked the teacher. 'Sometimes', said Ratnam. 'What do you make them out of?' asked the teacher. 'Any old scraps – things that don't seem of any use to anyone. Sticks and stones and bits of rubbish.' 'Well', said the teacher, 'I think you've probably got some good ideas there. How about teaching the other boys to make things too? Perhaps together we could think of a lot more things to make.'

So they began a club at Ratnam's school for making things out of scrap materials. Three days a week, for an hour after school, the club met, with Ratnam as one of the keenest members. It was amazing how many things they found they could make. They made toys of all kinds – kites and catapults, toy cars and helicopters, dolls' houses and dolls' chairs. They learned to make useful things too – hair pins out of old wire, spoons out of tin cans, leaf-plates and yards and yards of rope.

All these things they were able to sell and so help to raise money for the church and the school.

When the other boys saw how clever he was with his hands, they soon realised that Ratnam was not a good-for-nothing after all. There were many useful things he could do. The teacher knew that too and when Ratnam began to enjoy teaching others at school, he began to enjoy learning things too. At last he settled down to learning to read and write and do sums, and he is becoming a clever boy. Just as Ratnam himself has made many good things out of unwanted scraps that seemed useless, so now at school God is able to make out of Ratnam, the rough diamond, a really bright and shining Indian jewel.

The House by the Sea

The Nest – that's what they call the pink and white house where Giorgio lives, right by the seaside in Southern Italy. From the windows of his bedroom Giorgio can see the sparkling blue waters of the Mediterranean Sea, coming splashing on to the black sand of the beach which belongs to his house. The sand is black, because not far away stands the giant mountain of Vesuvius, which sometimes used to erupt in a great volcano, pouring black dust, called lava, over all the beaches down below. The black sand is usually burning hot to walk upon, because in summer the sun shines straight down from a cloudless sky on to this part of the Bay of Naples. Giorgio often runs as quickly as he can down the steps of his house, hopping across the black sand so as not to burn his feet too much, and then splashing into the beautiful cool waters of the bay, and calling to the other boys from the house to come down and play with him in the sea.

There are many boys living in the same building as Giorgio, but not all of them live in The Nest. There are other parts of the house which also look out on to the sea, where some of Giorgio's 220 brothers and sisters live. That sounds like a very big family, doesn't it?

They are the family who belong to the Casa Materna, the 'Mother House', which for over 50 years has been home for over 9,000 Italian boys and girls who have had no other home to look after them. Casa Materna is a splendid place to live in. Once it belonged to a wealthy prince, and was the special place he went to for his summer holidays. But now it belongs to a man called Dr. Santi who makes it a very special place for his large family of homeless Italian children all the year round.

The Nest is the part of the house where the smallest children live, and that is why Giorgio lives there, because for quite a long time he and his twin sister Violetta were the youngest members of the Casa Materna family. In fact, they first came there to live when they were small babies, so they cannot remember any other home at all. That is perhaps a good thing, for their first home was a sad place. They were born in a refugee camp, because their mother and father had no house to live in and no money to keep them with. They could not stay with their parents for very long because their mother had such a bad cough that the camp doctor said the babies must be kept away from her in case they caught the bad cough too. So the people who looked after the refugee camp had to find somewhere for the twins to go where they could be properly cared for. Straight away, they thought of Casa Materna and Dr. Santi, and wrote to ask him whether he could find room in his family for Giorgio and Violetta.

Somehow, although Dr. Santi's house at Casa Materna is always full of children, he can usually find room for some more. There are times when he feels he really ought to say, 'I'm sorry we have no room here for any more', but when he sees little babies like Giorgio and Violetta he finds he just can't say 'No' and he has to find room for them somewhere. He always remembers the words which are written up in great letters on the walls of Casa Materna, in Italian, so that all the people who pass by can understand them – *Lasciate i fanciulli venire a me* which means 'Let the children come to Me'. They are the words of Jesus, and they became the motto of Dr. Santi's father many years ago. He was a minister in Naples and one day when he was walking through the streets of that great city, he saw two little ragged children trying to sell matches to get some money. At first he walked past them, but then he seemed to hear the voice of Jesus saying to him, 'Those children are Mine and I want you to take care of them for Me.' So old Papa Santi took the children home with him to look after them and love them. Soon, other children came to join his family and he needed a bigger house to put them all in. At last, he managed to get Casa Materna as a home, and ever since then he has tried to bring as many little children as he can into the care of that family. His son now looks after the house, but he has gone on being true to his father's motto 'Let the children come to Me.'

So that's how Giorgio and Violetta came to The Nest even before they were old enough to understand what it was all about. What they could understand was that here they had comfortable cots to sleep in and good food to eat and a kind uncle to cuddle them whenever they felt a bit lonely or sad. Even these things are a bit puzzling to some of the children who come to The Nest when they are a bit bigger than the twins were and have not been used to being properly looked after. One little boy, who was tucked up carefully into a warm cot when he first arrived at The Nest, climbed out during the night and disappeared from the house. When Dr. Santi went to look for him, he found him lying outside on the pavement, because in the slums of Naples where he had lived before he had never slept anywhere else but on the pavement and couldn't get used to being in a bed! Another little girl was very surprised when she was given spaghetti and meat and tomatoes for dinner on her first day at The Nest, because before she came there she had only ever had tomatoes as a very special treat for her birthday, and had never had meat at all.

Meal-times are always a very happy time at Casa Materna, and as soon as Giorgio and Violetta were old enough, they joined all the rest of the big family in the dining-room in the big basement of the house. There, all the children from The Nest have their own special table, just near the table where Dr. Santi and all his helpers sit, so that at the end of the meal, the little ones can go over and climb up on the grown-ups' laps and finish it all off with some sweets and a story and perhaps even a few songs.

Everyone always seems to be singing at Casa Materna and Giorgio and Violetta have been quick to learn the lovely Italian songs which the children's choir sing. Giorgio especially has a very sweet voice, and often sings in the House Concerts, when the big boys blow on their bugles and bang on their drums in the School Band, and the little boys and girls sing songs and recite poems they have learnt in the primary school.

The concert which Giorgio likes best of all is the one that they have at Christmas. The children do a play which tells how once a man at a big house said he had no room for a man and his wife, and how they went into a stable where the Baby Jesus was born. Then the little ones sing a carol for the Baby Jesus round the great Christmas tree, where there is always a present for everyone. Then they play and sing and eat until they are too tired and too full to do any more. So the little ones go to bed, to be tucked up snugly in The Nest, where Giorgio and Violetta and many other children are now so happy, because they know that this is their home and there is room for them all.

Dancing in the Dark

Whenever Bapala heard the xylophone playing, she always wanted to dance. She would listen carefully first to make sure just where the sound was coming from, and then she would run as quickly as she could in that direction to join in all the fun with the other children. Usually, the boys were playing the xylophone in the small courtyard just outside her home which was in a village in Northern Ghana. To get there, she had to feel her way out of the little room where she lived with her mother and brothers and sisters and then along the dark passageway which linked together the rooms where other families lived, and out into the open courtyard where the women were working and where the children could all play together.

Bapala was nearly always the first to arrive. She could run very quickly, even though the passageway was so dark. All the other children had to grope their way through by feeling with their hands along the rough mud walls, but Bapala would run straight ahead, never needing to feel her way, because she was quite used to running in the dark. In fact, all the world was dark to Bapala. Ever since she was a baby she had been quite, quite blind.

That did not stop her from enjoying music. That was why she liked best of all the times when all the children were dancing and the xylophone was playing, because she could join in just like everybody else. She could dance very well, thudding her bare feet into the hard ground in time to the rhythm and clapping her hands and singing for joy, as she felt the sun shining down on her skin, even though she couldn't see its light.

Sometimes, after they had been dancing for a long time, the children would all sit down for a rest, and Bapala would sit chatting with them all, and cracking monkey nuts with them, which they all liked eating very much. But soon someone would say 'Let's go down to the pool for a swim' and then it wasn't so easy for Bapala. To get to the pool, the children had to go right away from their houses, and climb over the big wall that surrounded them and go out through the village down to the pool. Bapala could climb over the wall easily enough. She was used to scrambling up the ladder made out of a tree trunk, and down the other side, but once she was out in the village she needed someone to lead her along so that she wouldn't bump into things or lose her way. The other children would usually feel rather sorry for her and stop to help her find her way to the pool, where she loved to splash and play in the cool water.

There were some things she just couldn't join in at all, and one of these was the most exciting of all the things happening in the village. Once a week Bapala could tell by the tunes the xylophone was playing that it was a special day for Bapala's village. The children would all be practising their special songs ready for the time when the teacher would arrive. She came every Thursday afternoon, and as soon as the children heard the sound of her car turning the corner from the main road on to the rough track leading up to their village, they would stop singing and dancing and go scampering off, clambering over the ladder and running through the village to meet the car. They were often so excited that Bapala was left behind in the rush, but she would follow on as well as she could, listening carefully for the sound of the car stopping and of greetings being said, and making her way to the big spreading tree where all the people were gathering for their weekly meeting with the teacher.

She came every week to hold lessons for all the people in the village, grown-ups and children. No one in Bapala's village had ever had the chance to go to school, but they were all very keen to learn, and they were delighted when the teacher promised that she would teach everyone to read and write. She brought big picture-charts with her to teach people to recognise their letters and soon nearly everyone in the village was learning to read. So when the teacher came, they all proudly took their books along with them and showed her how much they could read and how well they were doing.

Poor Bapala! She would sit outside the big circle of the class having their reading lesson and she would wish so much that she could join in. But it was no good anyone giving her a book to read or a blackboard and chalk to write with. She couldn't see anything at all.

She could listen, though, and she did listen hard to all the stories the children were reading and all the songs they were learning to sing. One of her favourite stories was a story about Jesus and how He helped a blind man to see. Bapala used to wish very much that Jesus could come to her village and help her to see like other children. The teacher used to notice her sitting there alone and she wished that she could do something to help her.

Then one day, at the end of the lesson, something very surprising happened. The teacher called Bapala over to her and said 'Bapala, how would you like to go to school and learn to read like all the other children?' Bapala's heart thumped hard with excitement but she couldn't find any words to say. She just hung her head shyly and wondered what kind of school could ever teach a blind girl to read. The teacher went on to explain that an African Christian teacher who had come to live in Northern Ghana had started a school specially for blind children at a place called Wa, which was not very far from Bapala's village. It was a boarding school, so it would mean Bapala going away from home to live, but she would be able to come home for the holidays.

Bapala hardly knew what to say. She was rather nervous about going away from home, but very excited at the thought of being able to learn like other children. So the teacher took her to the chief of the village and asked him whether he would let Bapala go. The chief had to think about it very hard and discuss it with Bapala's mother, but in the end he agreed.

So one day, the xylophone playing in the courtyard

sounded especially exciting. It was the day when Bapala's lorry was due to arrive, to take her off to school. The chief helped to lift her into the lorry and all the children came to wave her off. Even though she couldn't see them, she was glad to hear them singing as she left, 'God be with you till we meet again'.

Bapala felt very shy when she first arrived at the School for the Blind. She didn't know her way about at all and she didn't know any of the other children. But she soon discovered one thing about them. All of them were blind, just as she was. It was the first time she had been just the same as everyone else. No one felt sorry for her, or treated her as though she were someone special. They all treated her just as though she were a normal person and could do everything they could do.

What a lot of things they could do! They brought their books to show to Bapala. Of course she couldn't see them at all, but that didn't matter with these books. She didn't have to see the letters; she could feel them with her fingers because the letters were made up of dots punched into large sheets of card. This is a special way of writing for blind people, which is called Braille. The other children soon helped Bapala to run her fingers over the cards and feel the different patterns of dots which made up the letters.

She learned to count too, with beads on frames. She learned geography with a big globe specially made where she could feel all the shapes of the countries. Bapala soon learned to recognise Africa, and then to find the part where the letters GHANA were written.

When it was time to go home for the holidays, Bapala was so excited that she could hardly wait to show the children back at home in the village all the things she had learned to do. Her chance came on the first morning she was back. As usual, as soon as the boys started playing the xylophone in the courtyard she was the first to be out there to join them in the dancing and the singing. Then when they stopped for a rest, Bapala picked up her book and started reading to them. She read her favourite story, about how Jesus helped the blind man to see. How surprised all the children were! Though Bapala's eyes were still blind, she had learned to see with her fingers and now, just like everyone else, she could read about the love of Jesus for herself.

The Big Black Box

Ever since Azariah had been a very little boy, the big black box had stood in the corner of the house where he lived with his mother and his four brothers in a small Indian town. It was the most important piece of furniture in their house. No-one was ever allowed to sit on it or use it as a table. It was always kept firmly locked and Azariah used to wonder what was in it. Perhaps there was some hidden treasure. Azariah's father, who had died when Azariah was a baby, had once been the keeper of the treasures in a Hindu temple, so perhaps he had put some of them there in that box. But if that was so, he wondered why his mother should still treasure it, because they had been Christians now for a long time and never went to the Hindu temple at all. Whenever Azariah asked his mother about it, she would shake her head and smile and say, 'One day, Azariah, when you are old enough to understand I will open the box and show you'.

That day came when Azariah was ten years old. He had always worked very hard at his lessons at the primary school. Sometimes the minister came to take a class, and Azariah always enjoyed those lessons. He and the minister became great friends.

No-one was really very surprised when it was announced that Azariah had passed an examination to go to a secondary school in the town of Dornakal, many miles away from his home. It meant he would have to live away at school during term-time, but his mother was proud that he had done so well and she agreed to let him go.

The night before he was due to leave home, she called him to her and said that she wanted to talk very seriously to him for a little while. She was going to show him what was in the big black box. Azariah's heart pounded with excitement as she put the key in the lock and scraped it round. Then the hinges creaked loudly as she pushed the lid open. It was too dark in the room to see what was inside, but his mother bent over the box and very tenderly brought out a long white gown and a plain, wooden cross. She handed them over to Azariah and said, 'That gown and that cross were all that your father possessed when he died. Once he had been a very wealthy man with a special job in the temple. But he decided to become a Christian and that meant that he lost his job and the money that went with it. His family would have nothing more to do with him, but he longed more than anything else to become a Christian minister. So he worked very hard at his books until he passed the examination to go to college and be trained. He became a very good minister and everybody in this town loved him. We were very, very happy in those days, and when you were born, your father said that he could not wish anything better for you than that one day you should become a minister too. He never lived to see you grow up, but now that you are going away from home I want you to take his gown and his cross away with you, always to remind you of him. Then I pray that one day you will wear his gown and carry his cross as a minister yourself'.

So Azariah took the box with him away to school, but he never told anyone its secret. The boys at school would have been very surprised if he had done so, because no-one could ever really imagine Azariah as a minister. In many ways, he was more like a comedian! One day when the teacher was late coming for a lesson, he went out to the front of the class and began imitating the headmaster so cleverly that everyone roared with laughter until suddenly the door opened and the head-master came in! There was a shocked silence. Azariah could not get back to his seat in time. He just stood there quivering, wondering what the headmaster would say. The headmaster had brought a special guest with him, Bishop Azariah of Dornakal. He called young Azariah over to introduce him to the bishop, saying, 'I don't know what you will think of your namesake, Sir; we just don't know what will become of him'. 'What do you want to be when you grow up?' the bishop asked him. 'I – I – think I shall go into my father's business,' Azariah stammered, but he never told anyone what his father's business had been.

When Azariah came home for the holidays, his mother began to wonder whether he ever would really be a minister. He never seemed to be serious for two minutes together. He was a terrible tease, and now that he was learning much more than his mother ever knew, he began to tease her too. He had been learning English at his new school, so he offered to teach his mother to speak English. 'You say exactly what I say,' he told her. Then he gave in English the following orders: 'Go to the door, call the sweetmeat man, buy yourself some sweetmeats,' and when his mother repeated the words after him, he hurried to obey her, even though she could not understand what she was saying!

Yet always in the evenings, after a day of fun and laughter, Azariah's mother and her sons would have a quiet time together in their home, singing together some of their Christian hymns which his father had once sung, and saying together the prayers he had taught them. At those family prayer times, it was usually Azariah who acted the part of the preacher, and his mother was always very glad when he read to them from the great black family Bible.

But as Azariah grew older, he began to wonder whether he really did want to be a minister after all. Sometimes when he was packing his books away in the big black box he would see his father's gown and cross lying there, and think that he would rather be a much richer man than his father had been. Someone suggested to him that he would make a very clever actor, and that was what he decided to do. He would go on the stage and become a famous man, and then perhaps later on, when he had made a lot of money, he would become a minister as well.

He was very happy when he was able to go on to the college, and begin there to prepare to be an actor. He used to be put in charge of the college concert. He loved to hear the audience laugh and clap when he was on the stage. It made him more determined than ever to be an actor. But one evening in the audience at the college concert, he recognised a familiar face. It was Bishop Azariah again. He remembered his young name-sake and came to see him after the show.

'Azariah', he said, 'When are you going to be about your father's business?'

The words stung like arrows in Azariah's heart. They reminded him of the story of how Jesus, when He was only twelve years old, decided that He must already start preparing Himself for the work God wanted Him to do. And in a flash, Azariah knew what he must do too. He must not wait any longer. He must begin straight away to prepare to carry on his father's work.

So the gown and the cross are not in the black box any longer. They are worn by Azariah who has gladly now become a minister of the gospel in the Church of South India.

The Big Idea

Janet was having a very special party. She didn't tell any of her friends what was going to happen. She just invited them all to come along at four o'clock on Saturday, October 24th to her home in North London. All her friends were very puzzled because they knew it was not Janet's birthday. It was still two months to Christmas. Then why was she holding a party?

John and Pat were the first two visitors to arrive. When John saw the table, all laden with cakes and jellies, he didn't bother to ask any questions. He wanted to start on the tea straight away. But Pat asked, 'What's the big idea Janet?' Janet just replied mysteriously, 'You wait and see'. By half-past four five people had come, all of them children from Janet's school, who were all mystified as to why they had been invited. 'Now that you're all here', said Janet, 'I'll explain. I have invited some very special visitors here today, but before they come, let me tell you now what the big idea is. It all began really the other day when I was coming home from school on the bus. It was a terribly wet day and we were stuck in the biggest traffic jam I have ever seen – we were held up all the way down the High Street and right beyond the bridge. I thought we would never get home! What made it worse, I was late already leaving school, and I knew Mother would be wondering where I'd got to.

'I asked the bus conductor how long he thought it would be before we got moving again,' and he said, 'It could be at least another half-hour, miss!' 'Half an hour!' I gasped. 'Why, I shall be in terrible trouble when I do get home.' 'Not half as much trouble as I shall be in', said the conductor. 'You, in trouble?' I asked. 'Whatever do you mean?' Then he explained to me that this was his last run of the day, and he had promised his little girl he would get home in time for tea, because it was her birthday and she wanted to have a party. She couldn't have a real party, he explained, because they had only just come to live in England and she didn't know anybody her own age. In any case there wasn't room in the place where they lived to invite people in. But her mother had bought a special cake and her father had promised to try and get home in good time for tea. 'But now I'm afraid it's all spoilt', he said, 'and Julie won't have her birthday tea after all.'

'I asked him to tell me about Julie, how old she was, and what school she went to. He said she was just about my age and he hoped to secure a place for her in our school at the beginning of next term. Meanwhile she was missing all her friends back at home in Jamaica very much indeed. He said the sun was nearly always shining there, and Julie loved to play on the beach and in the sea with crowds of other children. Ever since she arrived in England it had been cold and wet and she had been so miserable, staying at home in their one little room and never wanting to go out at all. 'I do wish she could find some friends here', he said.

'All the way home I couldn't stop thinking about Julie and how horrid it must be to live in a strange country without any friends. So when I got home and told Mummy about it, she said, 'Well, why not invite her to come here and have tea with you?' Then I had an even better idea. 'Couldn't I have a party especially to welcome her and invite some other children from overseas as well? There must be others around here just as lonely as she is. It would be such fun to get to know them. So that's why we're having this party today. Any minute now, our special visitors will arrive and we're going to give them a real welcome.'

Just at that moment the front door bell rang and all the children looked at each other in excitement. Janet ran to answer the door and the others could hear her welcoming the newcomers. First came Julie, who looked very pretty indeed in a pink party dress which suited her dark brown skin so well. Her black curly hair was tied in neat little plaits with big pink hair ribbons. Soon after her came Joe and Lee, two Chinese boys. Janet had met them when she and her mother had been out for a meal at the Chinese restaurant in the High Street.

At first, the children were very shy, but John soon thought of a way to break the ice. 'Let's start tea', he said, and soon all the children were settled round the table ready to tuck in. Joe and Lee had brought some special Chinese sweetmeats with them, which were really delicious. John said he couldn't decide which he liked best, the sweetmeats or the jellies, so he had large helpings of both!

While they were having tea, two more visitors arrived. They were Kofi and Anna from Ghana whose mother was studying in England and who went to Janet's church.

So now the party was complete – six English children and six children from overseas. After tea, Janet's Daddy suggested that they should have a quiz to find out how much they knew about each other's countries. The overseas children won that easily, because they knew far more about England than the English children did about Jamaica and Ghana and China. In fact, Daddy brought out a big map so that the overseas children could show the others exactly where their own countries were. Pat said that was a much more interesting geography lesson than they ever had at school!

Then it was time to play games. Kofi asked whether they could play a game the children always enjoyed in Ghana. One of the boys would pretend to be a snake, curled up by a make-believe tree in the corner of the room. The others would creep up and tease him until he reached out and caught one of them. Then the caught one joined on to the snake so that the snake grew longer and longer until everyone had been caught. That was a really hilarious game, with the snake in the end stretch-ing right up the stairs to catch his last victim!

After that, Mother suggested a sing-song. Julie said she could sing a special West Indian kind of song men sing when they are working in the sugar-fields. They tell each other all the news of the day in the words of

a special song called a calypso. She and her Daddy had
made up a calypso for Janet's party.

> England is a cold place
> And the skies are often grey
> And we were feeling lonely
> Till Janet came our way
> She made us feel so welcome
> She invited us to tea
> Because she had the big idea
> That we're all one family
> The big idea, the big idea
> We're all one family.

Everyone was joining in the chorus very heartily when
the telephone rang. It was John's mother ringing to
say that she would be late coming to pick him up in
the car. 'Don't you worry, Mum,' he said. 'We're having
a smashing party. Janet's invited lots of new friends –
and we've played new games and learned new songs
and even eaten new kinds of food! It's the best party
I've ever been to.'

By the time John's mother did arrive, all the other
children were leaving. 'See you again soon', they shouted
as they waved goodbye. John's mother looked after
them in surprise. When they'd gone, she said, 'But John,
you didn't tell me that Janet's new friends were coloured
children.' 'Didn't I, Mum?' he asked. 'Well, I suppose
I just didn't think it mattered.' 'Of course it doesn't,'
said Janet. 'You see, that's the big idea.'

The Newspaper Seller

'Read all about it!' shouted Chu En as loudly as he could, trying to make his voice heard over all the roar of the traffic in Hong Kong's busy streets. 'Read the latest news – books, magazines, papers for sale!' The louder he shouted, the more papers he would sell; the more papers he sold the more cents he would earn; the more cents he earned, the more food he could eat. That was a good enough reason to make any hungry boy work hard, and Chu En almost always was hungry, so he always worked as hard as he could.

Yet he usually had plenty of papers left at the end of the day. There were so many other boys selling papers on the same street, and there was always such a busy, bustling crowd of people passing by, jostling each other off the pavement, pushing past the newspaper-sellers, knocking over the magazine rack, that hardly anyone had time to stop and buy papers. Sometimes children would come, trying to peep at the comics on his rack without actually buying them, but then Chu En would charge them five cents a look, and they would sit down on the doorstep by his pitch and share the comic between them. At the end of the day, Chu En would gather up the papers he had left, and the money he had earned and take them home to his parents.

He knew that they would both be glad he had brought some papers home, but for quite different reasons. Father always liked to read them himself. Once, he had had many books to read, but they had all been left behind in China, when his family had fled away to Hong Kong, and now he was always eager to read anything that came his way. So he would take out his thick-lensed spectacles with their thin wire rims and peer through them to read all the latest news. Mother liked the newspapers for quite another reason. They helped to keep the family warm! There could sometimes be a chilly wind blowing even in Hong Kong, and although it never brought snow, it would whistle through all the cracks in their little shack, which was made out of only a few pieces of wood nailed together and propped up against the side of a rocky hill. So mother would stuff some of the newspapers into the holes in the walls and use others to put under Chu En's younger brother and baby sister to keep them warm as they dropped off to sleep on the floor. Then, sitting right underneath the little oil lamp which was the only light they had, she would carry on with her embroidery hoping to be able to sell it to make money to buy the food for the family.

They needed money. For many months, Father had been unable to find any work and now he had such a bad cough that he needed medicine urgently. That was why Chu En had to go out selling papers, instead of going to school.

The day was always a very long one for Chu En.

Every other day he had to be up early to try to get to the front of the queue at the water-tap down the street, which was turned on for only a few hours every second day and which had to be shared by so many families that they were allowed only one bucket each. Then he had to go off down Hung Hom hill where their shack stood packed in among thousands of others, down into the city streets below, to borrow the old bicycle he managed to rent for an hour each day so that he could deliver his newspapers to the big, suburban houses where the wealthy people lived.

He was out on that paper round not far from his home on the day when the disaster happened. The first he knew of it was when a taxi driver shouted, 'There's a big fire on Hung Hom hill.' He looked up and saw smoke in the sky. As quickly as he could, he raced back, past all the big shops, up the crooked, twisting back streets, till he could see his own hillside with the smoke and flames rising from the burning shacks. He ran up towards the place where his own shack stood, with his heart pounding wildly, wondering whether he would be in time to save his family. The firemen were there before him fighting with their long hoses to put out the flames, but it was a losing battle. All the wood and paper that the shacks were built of were so dry that the flames which had begun when someone knocked over an oil-lamp swept through them.

Fighting his way through the crowd Chu En searched through the black smoke for any sign of his mother and father. Then he saw them, struggling along, Mother carrying the baby and dragging his young brother behind her and trying to help Father as he staggered through the smoke coughing badly and saying over and over again, 'Whatever will become of us? Whatever shall we do?'

That was the question everyone was asking, even after the flames were all out and the fire had died down. Only the smouldering ruins of a thousand homes were left, and over five thousand more people in Hong Kong were homeless.

'Read all about it!' shouted Chu En again on the streets that evening. 'Read all about the great fire'. Some people stopped to buy a paper to find out what it was all about, but not many people cared. There were far too many fires in Hong Kong for people to worry too much about this one. So that night, Chu En needed even more of his papers than usual, as he and his family lay down to sleep in the doorway of the shop near where his paper-pitch stood, which was now their only house.

The next day, while Chu En was selling his papers, he found that there were some people who did care. A man who stopped to buy a paper asked him where he was living. He pointed to the doorway, and explained that his home had been burnt down. The man asked if he might go and meet Chu En's family, because he was a Christian minister and wanted to do all he could to help them.

He pointed out to Chu En's father a passage in the paper which said that the Government was planning to clear the hillside where the fire had been and build there blocks of concrete flats, with room for 2,000 people in each. 'Perhaps you will find a home there', he said. 'Meanwhile, we must try to make that cough of yours better and see if we can find some good food for the children.' He told Chu En's mother to come along to a clinic in the town, where the doctor would give her medicine for her husband and milk for the children.

It was many months before the one room flats were ready. Chu En's family managed to find a room for themselves, seven storeys up, right under the flat roof. Mother was so pleased with it that she gave it a special Chinese name meaning 'Sea-View', because from that height there was a lovely view of the blue waters of the harbour down below with all the big ships and the splendid buildings which make tourists think that Hong Kong is such a beautiful place.

Life in the resettlement building brought many changes for Chu En. The biggest surprise of all was that not long after his family moved there the Christian people came there too to start a school on the roof-top for all the children of the flats. Chu En's little brother was able to go there every day and at school he was given free milk to drink and good food to eat. Chu En was told that he could have a chance to learn too, for the teacher promised to hold evening classes for the paper boys and those like them who had to work all day.

Sometimes Chu En wonders what it is that makes these Christian people care about him and his family so much. He asked his teacher that once. He said it was because Jesus had told His followers to take the good news of His love to everyone and to preach it everywhere, even on the roof-tops!

The Harvest Envelope

The minister was growing very tired of addressing envelopes. There were so many of them to do. Every member of his church expected to receive his own envelope for the Harvest Festival Sunday, so that he could put his own special gift into it. That meant writing all the members' names on hundreds of envelopes, and taking them out to homes scattered all over the town, and some of them a long way out in the country. In the West Indian island where the minister lived some people had a very long way to go to church, but they would be disappointed if the minister failed to send them an envelope. So he decided he must get them all addressed and distributed by Saturday afternoon.

By the time Saturday came, there were still a lot of envelopes lying on his desk, waiting to be taken round. What was worse, it was raining, and in the West Indies when it rains, it really does rain. The water was just flowing down, so that the streets were all thick with mud and they looked as though they would never be dry again.

Inside the church, the people were getting ready for the Harvest Festival services. Some of them had brought great long sugar canes which they had cut down in the fields outside and which they now tied to the pillars and branched over to form arches all down the aisles of the church. Some of them had brought flowers from their gardens – deep pink poinsettias and purple bouganvillia. There were great bunches of bananas hanging from the pulpit, with the huge leaves of the banana tree making a deep green background for them. There were coconuts, and oranges and all kinds of other fruits which grow in the warm tropical climate of the West Indies.

The women who were working hard to decorate the church had nearly finished and the minister looked in to admire the result of their efforts. 'There's one thing we mustn't forget,' said one of the women. 'The plate by the door.' So they fetched the large brass plate to put it where everyone would see it as they came into the church. 'That's where they will put their gift envelopes,' she said.

Then the minister remembered that there were still a lot more envelopes to give out. But outside it was still raining hard, and he didn't know the way to find all the addresses. It would be a dreary business, tramping through the mud trying to find so many different families. However, he had better get on with it.

'Can I help you sir?' piped up a little voice just as the minister was going through the doorway. There stood Ebenezer, a young boy who came to the Sunday School. He was already quite wet through, because he had no coat, but only a patched shirt and ragged trousers and bare feet. The minister knew that he was from a very poor home. He lived with his grandmother, and she

never had very much money, not nearly enough to buy
Ebenezer any new clothes. But he never seemed to
grumble. Even now, in the pouring rain, he had a
bright, broad grin and was ready for anything.

'I'll take the envelopes for you, sir,' he said. 'I can
dart in and out between the showers, and I don't mind
splashing through the mud and getting wet.'

So he checked through all the names with the minister,
and found that he knew many of them very easily. Some
he was not so sure about. Some he didn't know at all,
but he would ask about them and see whether he could
find them.

He was gone for a very long time. In fact, it was dark
when he got back, and that was the only reason why he
had given up. He had found all but three of the names
on his envelopes. The minister was very grateful to him
indeed and wanted to give him a reward. 'Here is fifty
cents,' he said, 'go and do what you like with it.'

'Fifty cents? All for me?' gasped Ebenezer, and his
big eyes opened wide as his broad grin spread over his
face. 'I've never had as much money as that in all my
life.'

'Well, then, be careful how you spend it', said the
minister. 'Don't eat too many sweets all at once or you'll
make yourself ill.'

The next day was Harvest Festival Sunday. The
church was full of people. Even the ones who lived
farthest away had come in specially, bringing in with
them their envelopes which somehow or other Ebenezer
must have managed to get to them. At the end of the
service, the plate at the back of the church was piled

high with gifts. As the minister shook hands with everyone going out of the church, he looked eagerly to find Ebenezer to show him how all the envelopes had come back, bringing so many gifts. But Ebenezer was not there. 'I expect he's having a lazy day today,' thought the minister. 'But I do wish he had remembered to come to the Harvest.'

In the afternoon there was a special service for the children and young people. Again the minister searched everywhere for Ebenezer, but he was nowhere to be seen. There were very many other children there, however, all looking very pretty, dressed up in their best clothes. After they had sung their first hymn they came in procession down the aisles, bringing their harvest gifts. First came the girls, in their frilly frocks with ribbons on their black curly hair, carrying with them gifts of oranges or bananas or fruits or flowers. Then came the boys, all looking very smart in clean white shirts and freshly-pressed shorts. Most of them were wearing sandals too – though the minister had noticed that many of them had come into Sunday School bare-footed, and only put their sandals on for the procession, because they wanted to keep them looking as smart and new as they could. At the back of the procession came one boy with a large card that he had painted himself, with the word 'HARVEST' printed down it in large letters, and the words 'Happiness', 'Adoration', 'Rejoicing', 'Victory', 'Enterprise', 'Satisfaction' and 'Thanksgiving' written alongside it. 'There's a boy who has caught the spirit of Harvest', thought the minister as he placed the card at the foot of the communion rail. Again he remembered

Ebenezer and wished that he were there too.

The other children continued with their procession round the church, singing and clapping as they went. Then, just when it was all nearly over, in crept Ebenezer. He didn't want the other children to see him, because he hadn't got a smart suit to wear, nor a clean shirt, nor even a pair of sandals. But he came shyly up the aisle, with his big broad grin and his bright brown eyes dancing with delight.

When he got to the communion rail, he put his hand into the pocket of his tattered trousers and drew out an envelope. The name the minister had written on it had been crossed out. It was one of those Ebenezer could not find the day before, but instead he had written, in large round handwriting, his own name. And inside he had put his own gift – the fifty cents the minister had given him. It was all he had, but he wanted to give it as his thankoffering for all that God had given him.